The Financial Story Of Bill Ackman

From High-Stakes Bets to Market Influence: The Journey of a Hedge Fund Titan

William T. Seward

Table Of Contents

Introduction
The Rise of a Financial Visionary
A Brief Overview of Ackman's Life and Career

Chapter One; Early Life and Education
The Harvard Years: Shaping a Financial Mind
Early Influences and Formative Experiences

Chapter Two; Beginnings on Wall Street
The Birth of Gotham Partners
Early Successes and Setbacks
The Collapse of Gotham Partners and Its Aftermath

Chapter Three; The Creation of Pershing Square Capital Management
Establishing a New Hedge Fund Vision

Early Wins and the Strategy Behind Pershing Square
Core Principles and Investment Philosophy

Chapter Four; The Herbalife Saga
The Short Bet that Shook the Market
The Public Battle with Carl Icahn
The Impact of the Herbalife Campaign on Ackman's Reputation
Lessons from a Decade-Long Fight

Chapter Five ; Triumphs and Failures: Iconic Investments
Turning the Tide with Target Corporation
The Rise and Fall of J.C. Penney
Canadian Pacific: A Successful Activist Campaign

Chapter Six; Navigating Financial Crises
The Impact of the Pandemic on Ackman's Portfolio

Bill Ackman's Risk Management Tactics in Volatile Times

Chapter Seven; Philosophy of Activist Investing
How Ackman Reshaped Corporate Governance
The Power of Public Relations in Activist Campaigns
Key Activist Campaigns: Winners and Losers

Chapter Eight; Ackman's Major Wins and Market Influence
Ackman's Influence on Corporate Strategy
Notable High-Return Investments

Chapter Nine; Personal Life and Philanthropy
Ackman's Commitment to Charity and Philanthropy
The Pershing Square Foundation: Vision, Mission, and Contributions

Balancing Wealth with Social Responsibility

Chapter Ten; Criticism and Controversies
Media Criticism and Public Backlash
The Ups and Downs of Ackman's Public Image
Reflecting on Mistakes and Learning from Failures

Chapter Eleven; Bill Ackman's Legacy and Future
What's Next for Pershing Square and Bill Ackman
Reflections on a Career Full of High Stakes
The Legacy of Ackman's Investment Strategies for Future Generations

Conclusion

Introduction

The Rise of a Financial Visionary

Bill Ackman stands as one of the most influential and often polarizing figures in modern finance. His journey from a young man with a vision to one of the most prominent hedge fund managers in the world is a story marked by ambition, risk-taking, and an unwavering belief in his strategies. Ackman's rise is not merely a tale of accumulating wealth but a demonstration of how conviction, coupled with meticulous research and a willingness to challenge the status quo, can lead to unprecedented success in the financial world.

Born into a family with a strong business background, Ackman's early life provided him with the foundational knowledge that would later shape his career. His education at Harvard University, where he earned both his undergraduate degree and MBA, further honed his analytical skills and laid the groundwork for his entry into the financial sector. It was here that he began to develop his unique approach to investing—one that would later define his career. Ackman's rise to prominence was anything but ordinary. He did not take the traditional path of quietly building a portfolio through conservative investments. Instead, he made bold, public bets that often pitted him against some of the most established figures and institutions in the industry. These high-stakes gambles, driven by deep conviction, are what set him apart and ultimately led to his status as a financial visionary.

A Brief Overview of Ackman's Life and Career

Bill Ackman was born on May 11, 1966, in Chappaqua, New York, into a family that was well-versed in the world of real estate. His father, Lawrence Ackman, was a prominent real estate financier, and it was from him that young Bill likely inherited his entrepreneurial spirit.

This environment nurtured his early interest in business and finance, leading him to pursue higher education at Harvard University. After completing his studies, Ackman wasted no time in entering the world of finance, launching his first investment firm, Gotham Partners, in 1992. Gotham Partners was the first real test of Ackman's investing acumen. The firm initially experienced success, but it eventually encountered significant challenges, leading to its dissolution. However, the lessons learned during this period were invaluable. Rather than being discouraged by failure, Ackman used this experience as a stepping stone, refining his investment philosophy and preparing for greater challenges ahead. In 2004, Ackman founded Pershing Square Capital Management, the hedge fund that would become synonymous with his name. At Pershing Square, Ackman pursued an activist investing strategy, where he took significant stakes in companies and pushed for changes he believed would unlock value for shareholders.

His approach was often aggressive and public, leading to high-profile battles with corporate management and other investors. Some of his most notable campaigns involved companies like Target, JCPenney, and Herbalife, each of which garnered significant media attention and solidified Ackman's reputation as a formidable force in the financial world. Bill Ackman's influence extends far beyond the confines of his hedge fund. He has played a pivotal role in popularizing activist investing, a strategy that involves taking large positions in companies and advocating for changes to improve their performance. This approach, while not without its critics, has reshaped the way investors interact with corporations. Ackman's willingness to publicly challenge corporate management and push for reforms has led to significant changes in the companies he targets, often benefiting shareholders and, at times, the broader market. Ackman's importance in modern finance is also underscored by his ability to foresee and capitalize on market trends. Whether it was his early bet on the subprime mortgage crisis or his successful short position during the COVID-19 pandemic, Ackman has demonstrated an uncanny ability to navigate complex financial environments. His actions have not only generated substantial returns for his investors but have also influenced market behavior and investor sentiment on a broader scale.

Moreover, Ackman's approach to philanthropy and his efforts to balance his financial success with social responsibility further distinguish him in the world of finance. Through the Pershing Square Foundation, Ackman has contributed to various causes, reflecting his belief that wealth should be used to effect positive change in society. This combination of financial acumen and social consciousness has made Ackman a unique figure in the investment community, one whose impact will likely be felt for generations to come. This book aims to provide a comprehensive examination of Bill Ackman's financial journey, from his early years to his current status as a titan of the hedge fund industry. It seeks to explore the strategies, decisions, and events that have defined his career, offering readers an in-depth look at the man behind the headlines. Through detailed analysis of his major investments, public battles, and the evolution of his investment philosophy, the book will shed light on the factors that have contributed to Ackman's success. In addition to chronicling Ackman's financial achievements, this book will also delve into the challenges and controversies that have accompanied his rise. By examining both his triumphs and setbacks, the book will provide a balanced view of Ackman's career, offering insights into the risks and rewards of his approach to investing.

The book is intended for a broad audience, including finance professionals, investors, students of business, and anyone interested in understanding the dynamics of modern finance through the lens of one of its most influential figures. Whether you are a seasoned investor looking to glean insights from Ackman's strategies or a novice seeking to understand the world of hedge funds, this book will serve as a valuable resource. Ultimately, the purpose of this book is not just to recount the events of Ackman's life but to analyze the lessons that can be learned from his experiences.

By exploring his successes and failures, the book aims to provide readers with a deeper understanding of the principles that drive successful investing and the complexities of navigating the financial world at the highest levels.

Chapter One; Early Life and Education

Bill Ackman's story begins with a family deeply rooted in the world of business and finance, providing him with a foundation that would later shape his illustrious career. Born on May 11, 1966, in Chappaqua, New York, Ackman grew up in a family that valued entrepreneurship and financial acumen. His father, Lawrence Ackman, was a prominent figure in the real estate industry, leading Ackman Brothers & Singer, a commercial real estate financing firm.

This environment, where discussions of business deals and financial strategies were commonplace, had a profound influence on young Bill. Growing up, Ackman was exposed to the principles of business at an early age. His father's involvement in real estate financing offered him a front-row seat to the intricacies of the financial world, where risk assessment, investment strategies, and deal-making were part of daily life. This early exposure played a crucial role in developing Ackman's understanding of the financial markets and the importance of strategic thinking. Despite the financial comfort of his upbringing, Ackman's family instilled in him a strong work ethic and a sense of responsibility. His parents emphasized the value of education and the importance of hard work in achieving success. This blend of privilege and discipline provided Ackman with both the opportunities and the mindset needed to excel in his future endeavors. From a young age, Ackman exhibited a keen interest in numbers and a natural aptitude for mathematics. He was curious about how businesses operated and was particularly intrigued by the concept of value creation—how companies could grow and thrive through smart management and strategic investments. This curiosity would later evolve into a full-fledged passion for finance, setting the stage for his academic pursuits and professional career.

The Harvard Years: Shaping a Financial Mind

Bill Ackman's academic journey took him to one of the most prestigious institutions in the world—Harvard University. It was here that Ackman's intellectual and financial talents were honed, laying the groundwork for his future success in the world of finance. He attended Harvard College, where he pursued a degree in Social Studies, an interdisciplinary field that combines economics, politics, and philosophy. This choice of major reflected Ackman's broad interests and his desire to understand the world from multiple perspectives.

At Harvard, Ackman was known for his analytical mind and his ability to grasp complex concepts quickly. He was not content with merely understanding the theories taught in class; he sought to apply them to real-world scenarios. This approach to learning was evident in his coursework and extracurricular activities, where he often engaged in debates and discussions that went beyond the classroom.

During his time at Harvard, Ackman was also involved in various student organizations, including the university's investment club. Here, he had the opportunity to engage with like-minded peers and explore his interest in finance more deeply. The investment club provided a platform for Ackman to discuss investment strategies, analyze market trends, and test his ideas in a collaborative environment. This experience was instrumental in shaping his early investment philosophy and gave him a taste of the challenges and rewards of the financial world. In 1988, Ackman graduated magna cum laude from Harvard College. However, his thirst for knowledge and his desire to excel in finance led him to continue his studies at Harvard Business School. During his time at Harvard Business School, Ackman further refined his skills, particularly in areas related to investment management and corporate finance. He was particularly influenced by his professors, who were experts in their fields and provided him with insights that would later become central to his investment strategies. At Harvard Business School, Ackman was exposed to the case study method, a teaching approach that emphasizes real-world problem-solving. This method resonated with Ackman, as it aligned with his practical approach to learning and investing. The case studies often involved analyzing companies, understanding their financial health, and making decisions based on data—a process that closely mirrored the work Ackman would later do as a hedge fund manager.

One of the key lessons Ackman learned during his time at Harvard Business School was the importance of thorough research and due diligence. He understood that successful investing required not just a good idea, but a deep understanding of the underlying fundamentals of a company and the market in which it operated. This emphasis on research would become a hallmark of Ackman's investment style, distinguishing him from many of his peers in the industry. In 1992, Ackman graduated from Harvard Business School with an MBA, ready to embark on a career that would soon see him become one of the most successful and controversial figures in modern finance.

Early Influences and Formative Experiences

While Ackman's formal education at Harvard played a significant role in shaping his financial mind, his early influences and formative experiences also had a profound impact on his career trajectory. These influences came from various sources, including his family, mentors, and personal experiences.

One of the most significant influences on Ackman's early career was his father, Lawrence Ackman. From him, Bill inherited not only a passion for business but also a strong sense of ethics and responsibility. His father's success in real estate financing demonstrated to Ackman the importance of integrity in business dealings—a principle that would guide him throughout his career, even as he navigated the often cutthroat world of hedge funds. Another formative influence was Ackman's exposure to the world of investing at a young age. As a teenager, Ackman began reading about famous investors and studying their strategies. He was particularly inspired by Warren Buffett, whose value investing philosophy resonated with Ackman's own belief in the importance of thorough research and long-term thinking. Buffett's emphasis on investing in companies with strong fundamentals and holding them for the long term would become a core component of

Ackman's own investment approach. In addition to these influences, Ackman's early experiences in the financial industry also shaped his career. After graduating from Harvard Business School, Ackman co-founded Gotham Partners, an investment firm that sought to apply the principles he had learned at Harvard to the real world.

While Gotham Partners eventually faced significant challenges and was dissolved, the experience provided Ackman with invaluable lessons about the realities of investing, the importance of risk management, and the need to adapt and learn from failures. These early influences and formative experiences were crucial in shaping Bill Ackman's approach to finance and investing. They provided him with the tools and mindset needed to navigate the complexities of the financial markets and laid the foundation for the successes and challenges that would define his career. In summary, Bill Ackman's early life and education were characterized by a combination of privilege, hard work, and a relentless pursuit of knowledge.

His upbringing in a business-oriented family, coupled with his academic experiences at Harvard, provided him with the skills and insights needed to become one of the most influential figures in modern finance. These formative years set the stage for a career marked by bold decisions, significant risks, and, ultimately, remarkable success.

Chapter Two; Beginnings on Wall Street

Bill Ackman's entry into Wall Street was marked by the ambition and determination that would come to define his career. After earning his MBA from Harvard Business School in 1992, Ackman was eager to put his education and ideas into practice. Wall Street, with its complex financial systems and high-stakes environment, was the perfect arena for a young, driven individual with big ambitions.

Ackman was not interested in following the traditional path of working for a large financial institution. Instead, he had his sights set on creating something of his own, a firm where he could implement his unique vision of investing. This desire for independence and control over his investments led Ackman to co-found his first investment firm, Gotham Partners, with fellow Harvard graduate David Berkowitz. The firm was named after New York City, often referred to as Gotham, symbolizing Ackman's deep connection to the city and its financial district. Gotham Partners was more than just a typical investment firm; it was the manifestation of Ackman's belief in a research-driven, activist approach to investing. At the age of 26, Ackman was ready to make his mark on Wall Street.

The Birth of Gotham Partners

Gotham Partners was founded in 1993 with an initial capital of $3 million, raised primarily from friends and family. The firm's strategy was centered around a value-oriented approach, focusing on identifying undervalued companies with potential for significant returns. However, Ackman's approach was not just about finding undervalued assets; it involved a more hands-on strategy, where the firm would take an active role in influencing the management and direction of the companies they invested in.

This activist approach would become a hallmark of Ackman's career. From the outset, Gotham Partners was different from many of the hedge funds operating at the time. Ackman and Berkowitz were committed to rigorous research and due diligence, often spending months analyzing a company before making an investment. This thorough approach was aimed at minimizing risk and ensuring that each investment was backed by solid fundamentals. Ackman's philosophy was rooted in the idea that deep understanding and strategic involvement could unlock value in ways that the broader market had overlooked. Gotham Partners quickly gained attention in the financial world for its bold and unconventional strategies.

The firm's investment in companies like Rockefeller Center and First Union Real Estate Equity and Mortgage Investments showcased its willingness to take on complex, high-profile deals. These early moves highlighted Ackman's confidence in his ability to navigate challenging situations and his belief in the power of strategic intervention.

Early Successes and Setbacks

In its early years, Gotham Partners experienced several notable successes. One of the firm's early wins was its investment in Rockefeller Center, a deal that involved purchasing distressed debt tied to the iconic New York property. Ackman saw an opportunity where others saw risk, and his bet paid off handsomely when the property's value rebounded, resulting in significant profits for the firm.

Another success came with Gotham's investment in First Union Real Estate Equity and Mortgage Investments. Ackman identified the company as being undervalued and in need of strategic changes. Gotham Partners accumulated a large stake in the company and pushed for changes in its management and operations. The strategy worked, and the company's stock price rose, benefiting Gotham Partners' investors.

However, the early years were not without challenges. One of the firm's more difficult investments was its involvement with a golf course development company. The investment, which was based on the expectation that the golf course would become a lucrative asset, did not perform as expected. The project encountered numerous delays and financial difficulties, ultimately resulting in a loss for Gotham Partners.

This experience was a harsh reminder for Ackman of the unpredictable nature of certain investments and the importance of thorough due diligence. As Gotham Partners grew, so did the complexity of its investments. The firm began to engage in more aggressive strategies, including the use of leverage and investments in riskier, more distressed assets. These strategies, while potentially lucrative, also exposed the firm to greater risks. Ackman's confidence in his research and his willingness to take on challenging situations were both a strength and a vulnerability. The early successes and setbacks of Gotham Partners provided Ackman with valuable lessons that would shape his future endeavors. One of the key takeaways from this period was the importance of thorough and comprehensive research. Ackman's commitment to deep analysis before making an investment decision was reaffirmed by the successes of Gotham's more calculated bets.

He learned that understanding every aspect of a company—its management, operations, financials, and market conditions—was crucial to making informed investment decisions. Another important lesson was the need for adaptability. The setbacks faced by Gotham Partners, particularly the failed golf course investment, highlighted the importance of being flexible and ready to pivot when an investment did not go as planned.

Ackman recognized that even the most well-researched investments could encounter unforeseen challenges, and it was essential to have a strategy for mitigating losses and managing risk. Moreover, the experiences at Gotham Partners reinforced Ackman's belief in the value of an activist approach to investing. He saw firsthand how taking an active role in the companies he invested in could lead to positive changes and increased shareholder value. This activist strategy, which involved pushing for changes in management, operations, or strategy, became a defining feature of Ackman's career and would later be a cornerstone of Pershing Square Capital Management.

The Collapse of Gotham Partners and Its Aftermath

Despite its early successes, Gotham Partners eventually faced significant challenges that led to its collapse. The firm's aggressive investment strategies, particularly its involvement in complex real estate deals and distressed assets, began to backfire. By the late 1990s, Gotham Partners was entangled in a series of legal battles and disputes with shareholders, particularly over its investments in real estate and golf course developments.

The situation came to a head when Gotham Partners became embroiled in a protracted legal battle over its involvement in a troubled golf course development company. The legal issues, combined with the poor performance of some of the firm's other investments, led to a loss of investor confidence. By 2002, Gotham Partners was facing significant financial pressure, and Ackman made the difficult decision to wind down the firm. The collapse of Gotham Partners was a humbling experience for Ackman. It marked a turning point in his career, forcing him to confront the limitations of his investment strategies and the risks of overreaching. However, rather than being deterred by this setback, Ackman used it as an opportunity to reflect and refine his approach to investing.

The aftermath of Gotham Partners' collapse was a period of introspection and rebuilding for Ackman. He recognized the need for a more disciplined approach to risk management and a greater emphasis on liquidity and transparency in his investments. These lessons would be instrumental in the creation of Pershing Square Capital Management, the hedge fund that would eventually catapult Ackman to the forefront of the financial world.

In conclusion, Bill Ackman's beginnings on Wall Street, marked by the rise and fall of Gotham Partners, were formative experiences that shaped his investment philosophy and approach to risk. The early successes and setbacks taught him the importance of thorough research, adaptability, and the value of an activist approach. The collapse of Gotham Partners, while a significant setback, provided Ackman with the insights and resilience needed to build a more successful and sustainable investment firm in the future. This period in his career was not just a prelude to greater achievements, but a crucible in which Ackman's skills and strategies were tested and refined, setting the stage for his later successes with Pershing Square.

Chapter Three; The Creation of Pershing Square Capital Management

The collapse of Gotham Partners in 2002 was a pivotal moment in Bill Ackman's career. It was a period of reflection, learning, and reinvention. Despite the setbacks and the challenges that led to the dissolution of Gotham, Ackman was undeterred in his ambition to succeed on Wall Street.

He took the lessons learned from Gotham's demise and set out to build a new firm, one that would not only correct the mistakes of the past but also push the boundaries of what a hedge fund could achieve. This marked the beginning of Pershing Square Capital Management, the firm that would redefine Ackman's career and leave a significant impact on the financial world. In 2004, Ackman founded Pershing Square Capital Management with $54 million of his own money and a few million more from close family and friends. The decision to use his own capital was both a practical necessity and a statement of intent. By putting his own money on the line, Ackman demonstrated his confidence in his investment strategies and his commitment to the firm's success. This was a clear departure from the model used by many hedge funds, where managers primarily relied on external capital. Pershing Square was named after Pershing Square in Los Angeles, a historic plaza known for its cultural significance and history of public gatherings and activism. The name was symbolic of Ackman's approach to investing—public, activist, and transformative. From the outset, Pershing Square was designed to be different from traditional hedge funds. Ackman envisioned a firm that would not just manage investments but actively engage with the companies it invested in, driving change and creating value through strategic interventions.

Establishing a New Hedge Fund Vision

Ackman's vision for Pershing Square was rooted in the concept of activist investing, a strategy that involves taking significant stakes in companies and pushing for changes that would unlock shareholder value. While activist investing was not new, Ackman's approach was unique in its intensity and public nature. He believed that by taking a public stance on the changes needed within a company, he could rally other shareholders and apply pressure on management to implement those changes.

One of the core components of Ackman's vision was transparency. He believed that transparency was key to gaining the trust of both his investors and the public. Unlike many hedge funds that operated in secrecy, Ackman was committed to being open about Pershing Square's investments, strategies, and objectives.

He regularly communicated with investors and the public, often through detailed letters and presentations that outlined his views on the companies in which Pershing Square was invested. This level of transparency was unusual in the hedge fund industry and set Pershing Square apart from its peers. Another key aspect of Ackman's vision was the concentration of his investments. While many hedge funds spread their bets across a wide range of assets to minimize risk, Ackman chose to focus on a smaller number of high-conviction investments. This approach allowed him to dedicate significant resources and attention to each investment, ensuring that Pershing Square could take a more active and influential role in shaping the outcomes of its investments.

Early Wins and the Strategy Behind Pershing Square

Pershing Square's early years were marked by a series of high-profile investments that showcased Ackman's activist strategy and his ability to generate significant returns for his investors. One of the first major successes was the investment in fast-food giant Wendy's. In 2005, Pershing Square acquired a substantial stake in Wendy's and began pushing for the company to spin off its Tim Hortons coffee chain, which Ackman believed was undervalued by the market.

After months of pressure, Wendy's agreed to the spin-off, and the move resulted in a substantial increase in shareholder value. The success of Wendy's campaign solidified Ackman's reputation as a formidable activist investor and demonstrated the effectiveness of his strategy. Following the success with Wendy's, Ackman continued to identify companies where he believed significant value could be unlocked through strategic changes. One such investment was in McDonald's. Ackman took a sizable stake in the fast-food giant and advocated for the company to return capital to shareholders through stock buybacks and to consider franchising a larger portion of its restaurants. While Ackman's proposals were met with resistance from McDonald's management, the company eventually adopted some of his suggestions, leading to improved financial performance and a rise in the stock price. Another early win for Pershing Square came with the investment in Target Corporation. In 2007, Ackman built a large position in the retailer and proposed a series of changes aimed at improving its operational efficiency and real estate strategy.

Although Ackman's campaign at Target was more contentious and ultimately less successful than some of his other investments, it demonstrated his willingness to take on large, established companies and push for significant changes. The Target campaign was a learning experience for Ackman, reinforcing the importance of understanding the nuances of each company's situation and the need for a tailored approach to activist investing. Throughout these early campaigns, Ackman's strategy was consistent: identify undervalued companies with strong fundamentals, take a significant stake, and advocate for changes that would unlock value. This strategy was not without risks, as it often put Ackman at odds with company management and exposed Pershing Square to significant volatility. However, the success of these early investments helped build the firm's reputation and attract additional capital from investors who were drawn to Ackman's bold and decisive approach.

Core Principles and Investment Philosophy

At the heart of Pershing Square's success is Ackman's investment philosophy, which is based on a set of core principles that guide the firm's decisions and strategies. One of the central tenets of Ackman's philosophy is the concept of value investing. Like Warren Buffett, one of his early influences, Ackman believes in investing in companies that are undervalued by the market but have strong fundamentals and long-term growth potential.

However, Ackman's approach differs from traditional value investing in that he is not content to simply hold these investments passively; he actively works to unlock value through strategic interventions. Another key principle of Ackman's philosophy is the importance of thorough research and due diligence. Ackman is known for his meticulous approach to analyzing companies, often spending months or even years studying a potential investment before committing capital. This deep research allows Ackman to identify opportunities that others might overlook and gives him the confidence to take bold positions in his investments. Ackman's research is not limited to financial statements and market data; he also takes into account the quality of a company's management, its competitive position, and its long-term strategic vision.

Ackman's focus on transparency is another core principle that sets Pershing Square apart. From the beginning, Ackman has been committed to being open and honest with his investors about the firm's strategies, risks, and performance. This transparency extends to his activist campaigns, where he often makes his case to the public through detailed presentations and media appearances.

Ackman believes that by being transparent, he can build trust with his investors and the broader market, which in turn helps to rally support for his campaigns. Risk management is also a critical component of Ackman's investment philosophy. While Pershing Square is known for taking concentrated positions in its investments, Ackman is acutely aware of the risks involved. He employs various strategies to manage and mitigate these risks, including the use of hedges and the careful selection of investments that have a margin of safety. Ackman's approach to risk management is informed by his experience with Gotham Partners, where the firm's aggressive strategies ultimately led to its downfall. At Pershing Square, Ackman has worked to strike a balance between taking bold positions and managing risk to protect his investors' capital.

Finally, Ackman's belief in the power of activism is central to his investment philosophy. He views activist investing not just as a way to generate returns, but as a means of driving positive change in the companies he invests in. Ackman believes that by pushing for better management, more efficient operations, and more effective capital allocation, he can create value not just for Pershing Square's investors, but for all shareholders.

This belief in the transformative potential of activism is what drives Ackman to take on challenging and often controversial campaigns, even when the odds seem stacked against him. In conclusion, the creation of Pershing Square Capital Management was a defining moment in Bill Ackman's career. Through his visionary approach to activist investing, his commitment to transparency, and his rigorous research and risk management, Ackman has built Pershing Square into one of the most successful and influential hedge funds in the world. The early wins achieved by the firm demonstrated the effectiveness of Ackman's strategies and established Pershing Square as a leader in the field of activist investing. Today, the core principles and investment philosophy that Ackman developed at Pershing Square continue to guide the firm's decisions and ensure its ongoing success in the ever-changing world of finance.

Chapter Four; The Herbalife Saga

The Herbalife saga stands as one of the most controversial and high-profile episodes in Bill Ackman's career. It is a story that exemplifies the risks, rewards, and challenges of activist investing on a grand scale. This saga, which began in 2012 and spanned nearly a decade, involved a multi-billion-dollar bet against a global nutrition company, a fierce public feud with fellow billionaire investor Carl Icahn, and a broader debate about the ethics of short-selling and corporate practices. For Ackman, the Herbalife campaign was not just an investment; it was a crusade driven by a deep conviction that he was on the right side of both finance and morality.

The Short Bet that Shook the Market

In December 2012, Bill Ackman made headlines by announcing that Pershing Square Capital Management had taken a massive short position in Herbalife Ltd., a global nutrition company that sells dietary supplements, weight management products, and personal care items. Ackman's short position, valued at over $1 billion, was based on his belief that Herbalife operated as a pyramid scheme—a business model that relies on recruiting new participants to generate income rather than selling actual products to end consumers. Ackman's thesis was rooted in the belief that Herbalife's business practices were deceptive and unsustainable. He argued that the company's primary source of revenue was the recruitment of new distributors rather than genuine product sales, and that the vast majority of these distributors lost money, while only a small fraction profited.

To support his claims, Ackman launched a comprehensive public relations campaign, which included a detailed presentation, media appearances, and even a website dedicated to exposing Herbalife's alleged wrongdoing. The presentation, titled "Who Wants to Be a Millionaire?", was a meticulously researched, multi-hour exposé that laid out Ackman's case against Herbalife. It accused the company of preying on vulnerable populations, particularly low-income and minority communities, by selling them a false dream of financial independence. Ackman's argument was that Herbalife's business model was not only illegal but also morally reprehensible, and he predicted that the company would eventually collapse under regulatory scrutiny, driving its stock price to zero.

The impact of Ackman's announcement was immediate and dramatic. Herbalife's stock price plummeted as investors reacted to the news, and the company found itself under intense scrutiny from both the media and regulators. The U.S. Federal Trade Commission (FTC) launched an investigation into Herbalife's practices, and the company was forced to defend itself against accusations of operating a pyramid scheme. The market was roiled by the sheer scale of Ackman's bet, and the saga quickly became a defining moment in the world of finance.

The Public Battle with Carl Icahn

As the Herbalife saga unfolded, it became clear that Ackman's campaign would not go unchallenged. One of the most significant and dramatic developments came in early 2013 when Carl Icahn, a fellow billionaire investor known for his own activist campaigns, took the opposite side of Ackman's trade. Icahn not only disagreed with Ackman's assessment of Herbalife but also saw an opportunity to profit from what he believed was a flawed bet. The feud between Ackman and Icahn quickly became personal and very public. The two engaged in a heated exchange on live television, with Icahn famously calling Ackman a "liar" and a "crybaby." The verbal sparring between the two titans of finance captivated the financial world and turned the Herbalife saga into a media spectacle. Icahn's involvement added a new layer of complexity to the situation, as he began buying up large amounts of Herbalife stock, ultimately becoming one of the company's largest shareholders. Icahn's support for Herbalife was not just a financial bet; it was also a direct challenge to Ackman's credibility and investment strategy. Icahn argued that Herbalife was a legitimate business and that Ackman's claims were baseless.

He accused Ackman of trying to manipulate the market for personal gain and vowed to hold his position in Herbalife as long as Ackman remained short. The public battle between these two high-profile investors drew attention from all corners of the financial world, with analysts, commentators, and the public closely watching each development. For Ackman, the feud with Icahn added another dimension to the already complex Herbalife saga. It was no longer just a battle over the financial health of a single company; it was also a clash of egos and investment philosophies. The stakes were incredibly high, not just in terms of money but also in terms of reputation and legacy. Ackman's commitment to his position was unwavering, even as Herbalife's stock price began to recover, fueled in part by Icahn's purchases and the company's aggressive defense.

The Impact of the Herbalife Campaign on Ackman's Reputation

The Herbalife saga had a profound impact on Bill Ackman's reputation, both within the financial industry and in the public eye. On one hand, Ackman's boldness in taking on a company as large and established as Herbalife, and his willingness to engage in a protracted public battle, solidified his status as one of the most prominent and fearless activist investors of his generation.

The campaign showcased Ackman's deep conviction in his research and his willingness to take significant risks based on that conviction. However, the prolonged nature of the campaign and the intense scrutiny that accompanied it also exposed Ackman to significant criticism. As the battle dragged on, with Herbalife's stock price stabilizing and even rising at times, some began to question the validity of Ackman's thesis. Critics argued that Ackman had overreached, allowing his personal animosity towards Herbalife and its management to cloud his judgment. The failure of Herbalife's stock to collapse, as Ackman had predicted, led to questions about whether he had miscalculated the strength of the company and the resilience of its business model.

The public nature of the campaign also meant that every development was closely watched and reported on, adding to the pressure on Ackman and his firm. As time went on, the media narrative began to shift from Ackman's initial claims of moral righteousness to a more critical view of his motivations and strategy. Some commentators suggested that Ackman's campaign against Herbalife was as much about his ego and desire to be proven right as it was about the financial merits of the trade.

Despite these challenges, Ackman remained committed to his position, even as the costs of the short bet mounted. By 2017, however, it became clear that the Herbalife campaign was not going to end in the decisive victory that Ackman had anticipated. Herbalife reached a settlement with the FTC that required changes to its business practices but stopped short of declaring the company a pyramid scheme. With the regulatory threat diminished and Herbalife's stock price buoyed by Icahn's continued support, Ackman eventually decided to exit his short position.

Lessons from a Decade-Long Fight

The Herbalife saga was a decade-long fight that offered numerous lessons for Bill Ackman and the broader financial community. One of the key lessons was the importance of timing and market sentiment in activist campaigns. While Ackman's research and arguments against Herbalife were thorough and compelling, the timing of the campaign and the resilience of Herbalife's stock price highlighted the challenges of betting against a company with strong market support and an influential backer like Carl Icahn.

Another lesson was the danger of letting personal emotions and public perception influence investment decisions. The public feud with Icahn, while dramatic and attention-grabbing, may have clouded Ackman's judgment and contributed to his reluctance to exit the position earlier. The saga underscored the need for discipline and objectivity in managing investments, especially in high-profile situations where emotions can run high. The Herbalife campaign also highlighted the risks and rewards of short-selling as a strategy. While short-selling can be highly profitable when successful, it is also inherently risky, as losses can be theoretically unlimited. The prolonged nature of the Herbalife short and the significant costs associated with maintaining the position were a reminder of the challenges involved in betting against a company, particularly one with a large and loyal shareholder base. Despite the outcome, the Herbalife saga did not diminish Ackman's reputation as a bold and innovative investor. If anything, it reinforced his image as a man willing to take on significant challenges, even in the face of adversity. The campaign also demonstrated Ackman's resilience and ability to navigate complex and contentious situations, qualities that would continue to define his career.

In conclusion, the Herbalife saga was a defining chapter in Bill Ackman's career. It was a story of conviction, conflict, and controversy that captivated the financial world and tested Ackman's mettle as an investor. While the campaign did not end in the clear victory that Ackman had hoped for, it provided valuable lessons about the complexities of activist investing, the importance of timing, and the need for objectivity in managing high-stakes positions. Ultimately, the Herbalife saga stands as a testament to the risks and rewards of pursuing bold, transformative investment strategies in the ever-volatile world of finance.

Chapter Five ; Triumphs and Failures: Iconic Investments

Bill Ackman's career is punctuated by a series of iconic investments that highlight both the triumphs and failures inherent in his bold, activist approach to investing. Each of these investments showcases Ackman's willingness to take significant risks, his deep conviction in his analysis, and his readiness to engage in public battles to push for change. From retail giants to pharmaceutical companies, Ackman's investments have not only impacted the companies involved but have also influenced broader market perceptions and practices. These investments, particularly in Target Corporation, JCPenney, Canadian Pacific, and Valeant Pharmaceuticals, provide a window into the strategies that define Ackman's career, as well as the challenges and rewards that come with high-stakes investing.

Turning the Tide with Target Corporation

In the mid-2000s, Bill Ackman turned his attention to Target Corporation, the retail giant known for its combination of low prices and high-quality goods. Ackman believed that Target was an undervalued asset and that significant value could be unlocked through strategic changes in the company's management and operations. In 2007, through Pershing Square, Ackman acquired a substantial stake in Target, making him one of the company's largest shareholders.

Ackman's strategy for Target was multifaceted. He proposed a series of changes aimed at improving the company's operational efficiency and enhancing shareholder value. One of his most controversial proposals was for Target to spin off its real estate assets into a separate entity, which he believed would unlock billions of dollars in value. Ackman argued that Target's real estate holdings were being undervalued by the market and that a spin-off would allow the company to focus more on its core retail business while also providing a significant return to shareholders. However, Ackman's campaign at Target was met with resistance from the company's management. The board and executive team were skeptical of Ackman's proposals, particularly the idea of spinning off the real estate assets, which they believed could destabilize the company's operations and financial health. The resistance from Target's management led to a public battle, with Ackman pushing for changes and the company pushing back. Despite his efforts, Ackman's campaign at Target ultimately did not achieve the success he had hoped for. The company's management refused to implement his proposed changes, and the spin-off of the real estate assets never materialized. By 2011, Pershing Square had exited its position in Target, with Ackman acknowledging that the investment had not delivered the returns he had anticipated. The Target campaign was a reminder of the challenges of activist investing, particularly when management is resistant to change.

The Rise and Fall of J.C. Penney

Perhaps one of the most high-profile and dramatic investments in Ackman's career was his involvement with J.C. Penney, the struggling department store chain. In 2010, Ackman saw an opportunity to turn around the ailing retailer, which had been losing market share to competitors like Walmart and Amazon. Through Pershing Square, Ackman acquired a significant stake in J.C. Penney, and he quickly set about implementing his vision for revitalizing the company.

Ackman's strategy for J.C. Penney involved a bold and ambitious transformation of the company's business model. He believed that the retailer needed to reinvent itself to survive in an increasingly competitive retail environment. To execute this transformation, Ackman brought in Ron Johnson, the former head of Apple's retail division, as the new CEO. Johnson was widely credited with the success of Apple's retail stores, and Ackman believed that he could bring the same level of innovation and customer focus to J.C. Penney.

Under Johnson's leadership, J.C. Penney embarked on a radical overhaul of its operations. The company eliminated its long-standing practice of offering discounts and sales, replacing them with a strategy of "everyday low prices." The store layouts were redesigned, and the product offerings were revamped to focus on higher-end, trendier merchandise. Ackman and Johnson hoped that these changes would attract a new, more affluent customer base and restore J.C. Penney's relevance in the retail market. However, the transformation of J.C. Penney did not go as planned. The changes alienated the company's core customer base, which had grown accustomed to the frequent discounts and promotions. Sales plummeted, and the company's financial performance deteriorated rapidly. The board of directors, increasingly concerned about the direction of the company, eventually decided to remove Johnson as

CEO in 2013, less than two years after he had taken the helm. For Ackman, the J.C. Penney investment was a significant setback. Despite his best efforts, the company's turnaround had failed, and Pershing Square ultimately sold its stake in the company at a substantial loss. The experience with J.C. Penney was a humbling one for Ackman, highlighting the risks of making sweeping changes to a company's business model and the importance of understanding and catering to the existing customer base. It also reinforced the idea that even the most well-intentioned and well-thought-out strategies can fail in the face of unforeseen challenges.

Canadian Pacific: A Successful Activist Campaign

In contrast to the challenges faced with Target and JCPenney, Ackman's investment in Canadian Pacific Railway (CP) is often cited as one of his most successful activist campaigns. In 2011, Ackman took a substantial position in Canadian Pacific, one of Canada's largest railway companies, which was underperforming compared to its peers. Ackman believed that the company's problems were largely due to inefficiencies in its operations and poor management. Ackman's strategy for Canadian Pacific was straightforward: replace the company's management with leaders who had a proven track record of success in the railway industry. To this end, Ackman identified Hunter Harrison, the former CEO of Canadian National Railway (CN), as the ideal candidate to lead the turnaround at Canadian Pacific. Harrison was widely respected in the industry for his ability to improve operational efficiency and drive profitability, and Ackman believed that his leadership could transform Canadian Pacific.

The campaign to install Harrison as CEO was not without its challenges. Ackman faced resistance from Canadian Pacific's board and existing management, who were reluctant to cede control of the company to an outsider. However, Ackman's persistence, coupled with strong support from other shareholders, eventually led to a proxy battle in which Ackman successfully ousted the existing board members and installed Harrison as CEO in 2012. Under Harrison's leadership, Canadian Pacific underwent a dramatic transformation. Harrison implemented a series of operational improvements that significantly increased the efficiency of the railway's operations. These changes included reducing train turnaround times, optimizing routing, and cutting costs across the board. The results were remarkable: Canadian Pacific's profitability soared, and its stock price more than tripled within a few years.

Ackman's success with Canadian Pacific was a testament to the power of effective leadership and the importance of operational efficiency in driving shareholder value. The investment not only delivered substantial returns for Pershing Square's investors but also solidified Ackman's reputation as a successful activist investor who could deliver results. The Canadian Pacific campaign remains one of the most prominent examples of how activist investing can create significant value when executed effectively.

One of the most complex and controversial investments in Ackman's career was his involvement with Valeant Pharmaceuticals. In 2015, Ackman took a significant stake in Valeant, a pharmaceutical company known for its aggressive acquisition strategy and controversial pricing practices. At the time, Valeant was one of the hottest stocks in the market, having delivered substantial returns to investors through its rapid growth and high margins. Ackman was initially attracted to Valeant because of its unique business model. Unlike traditional pharmaceutical companies that invest heavily in research and development, Valeant focused on acquiring existing drugs and raising their prices to maximize profitability. Ackman believed that this model, combined with the company's ability to identify and acquire undervalued assets, would continue to generate significant returns for shareholders. However, shortly after Ackman's investment, Valeant became embroiled in a series of scandals that would ultimately lead to its downfall. The company faced accusations of price gouging, improper accounting practices, and unethical business behavior. These issues came to a head in late 2015 when it was revealed that Valeant had been using a specialty pharmacy called Philidor to inflate its sales and manipulate insurance reimbursements.

The fallout from these revelations was swift and severe. Valeant's stock price plummeted, and the company found itself under investigation by multiple regulatory agencies. As the crisis deepened, Ackman took an increasingly active role in trying to stabilize the company. He joined Valeant's board of directors and worked to implement changes aimed at restoring investor confidence, including replacing the CEO and overhauling the company's governance practices. Despite Ackman's efforts, Valeant's problems proved too deep-rooted to be resolved quickly. The company's financial performance continued to deteriorate, and its stock price remained under pressure. In 2017, after two years of trying to turn the company around, Ackman made the difficult decision to sell Pershing Square's stake in Valeant at a substantial loss. The investment in Valeant was one of the most significant failures of Ackman's career, resulting in billions of dollars in losses for his investors. The Valeant experience was a sobering one for Ackman, highlighting the risks associated with investing in companies with aggressive business models and questionable practices. It also underscored the importance of due diligence and the need to thoroughly understand a company's operations and ethical standards before making a significant investment. Despite the setback, Ackman remained committed to his investment philosophy, viewing the experience as a learning opportunity that would inform his future decisions.

Bill Ackman's career is a testament to the complexities of high-stakes investing. His triumphs and failures in investments like Target, JCPenney, Canadian Pacific, and Valeant Pharmaceuticals illustrate the challenges of activist investing and the high rewards and significant risks that come with bold, transformative strategies. Ackman's triumphs, such as the turnaround at Canadian Pacific, showcase the potential for activist investors to create substantial value when they identify the right opportunities and implement effective changes. The Canadian Pacific campaign, in particular, is a model of how strategic leadership and operational efficiency can transform an underperforming company into a market leader. Ackman's success with Canadian Pacific not only delivered significant returns for Pershing Square's investors but also reinforced his reputation as one of the most effective activist investors of his generation. On the other hand, Ackman's experiences with Target, JCPenney, and Valeant Pharmaceuticals highlight the challenges and pitfalls of activist investing. The Target campaign, while grounded in solid financial analysis, ultimately failed due to management resistance and the complexity of executing a large-scale real estate spin-off.

The J.C. Penney investment, despite its initial promise, fell apart due to the misalignment between the company's new strategy and the needs of its existing customer base. And the Valeant debacle serves as a cautionary tale about the dangers of investing in companies with questionable business practices and the difficulty of reversing a downward spiral once a company's reputation is tarnished. These investments underscore the importance of timing, market dynamics, and the ability to adapt strategies as circumstances change. In the case of Valeant, the speed at which the company's fortunes deteriorated caught many, including Ackman, by surprise. It also highlighted the risks associated with heavily concentrated positions in volatile industries like pharmaceuticals, where regulatory scrutiny and public perception can rapidly shift.

For Ackman, each of these iconic investments offered lessons that would shape his approach to future opportunities. The successes reinforced his belief in the power of activism and the importance of thorough research, while the failures taught him the necessity of flexibility, humility, and the need to manage risk more carefully. Ackman's willingness to learn from both his triumphs and setbacks is a testament to his resilience and his commitment to evolving as an investor.

In the broader context of the financial world, Ackman's iconic investments have also contributed to the ongoing debate about the role of activist investors in shaping corporate governance. His campaigns have shown that while activist investors can drive significant positive change, their interventions can also be disruptive and, at times, controversial. Ackman's career illustrates that the line between success and failure in activist investing is often thin, and the outcomes can hinge on factors beyond the investor's control, such as market conditions, regulatory actions, and the reactions of company management. In summary, Bill Ackman's iconic investments in Target, JCPenney, Canadian Pacific, and Valeant Pharmaceuticals encapsulate the highs and lows of his career as an activist investor. These investments, each with their own unique challenges and outcomes, reflect the complexity of the investment world and the fine balance between risk and reward. For Ackman, these experiences have not only defined his career but have also provided valuable lessons that continue to inform his approach to investing. Whether in success or failure, Ackman's journey through these iconic investments offers insights into the intricate dance of strategy, execution, and adaptation that defines the world of high-stakes finance.

Chapter Six; Navigating Financial Crises

Bill Ackman's career has been defined not only by bold bets and high-profile activist campaigns but also by his ability to navigate through financial crises. His success in weathering these storms can be attributed to his sharp analytical skills, strategic foresight, and willingness to take decisive action in the face of uncertainty. Whether during the 2008 financial crisis or the global COVID-19 pandemic, Ackman's ability to read the market and manage risk has allowed him to emerge stronger in some of the most challenging times in financial history.

His navigation of these crises reveals not only his skill as an investor but also his resilience in volatile times. The 2008 financial crisis was a significant turning point for many investors, and Ackman was no exception. As the U.S. housing market collapsed, the global economy spiraled into one of the worst recessions since the Great Depression. Many financial institutions and hedge funds saw massive losses, and the crisis left few areas of the market untouched. However, unlike many of his peers, Ackman managed to weather the storm and even find opportunities in the turmoil. His success during this period can be traced to his early recognition of the systemic risks in the housing market and his contrarian approach to investing. Well before the crisis hit, Ackman had been warning about the dangers of over-leverage in the financial system and the unsustainable practices in the mortgage industry. One of Ackman's most notable moves during the 2008 financial crisis was his bet against bond insurer MBIA (Municipal Bond Insurance Association). Ackman believed that MBIA was dangerously exposed to the risks of the subprime mortgage market and that the company's assurances to investors were unfounded.

He began shorting MBIA's stock in the mid-2000s, long before the financial crisis unfolded. Ackman publicly criticized the company's practices, arguing that its exposure to mortgage-backed securities made it vulnerable to collapse. When the housing market finally imploded in 2007-2008, MBIA's stock plummeted, validating Ackman's thesis. His short position against the company paid off handsomely, earning Pershing Square hundreds of millions of dollars. Ackman's ability to foresee the collapse of MBIA and take action against it not only preserved his firm during the financial crisis but also cemented his reputation as a prescient investor willing to go against the grain.

The Impact of the Pandemic on Ackman's Portfolio

More than a decade after the 2008 financial crisis, Ackman would once again find himself navigating another global economic upheaval—this time triggered by the COVID-19 pandemic. As the virus spread rapidly around the globe in early 2020, financial markets were thrown into chaos. Entire industries, from travel to hospitality, ground to a halt, and global economies faced an unprecedented shock.

For investors, the pandemic presented both immense challenges and opportunities, and Ackman proved once again that he had the ability to act decisively in a crisis. The pandemic's initial impact on Ackman's portfolio was significant. Several of Pershing Square's largest investments, including positions in companies such as Hilton Worldwide and restaurant chain Chipotle, were directly affected by the lockdowns and travel restrictions imposed to slow the spread of the virus. The hotel and restaurant industries were among the hardest hit, as travel came to a standstill and consumer behavior shifted dramatically. Ackman, however, did not sit idly by as the pandemic unfolded. Recognizing the gravity of the situation early on, he took swift and aggressive action to protect Pershing Square's portfolio.

In February 2020, as markets began to show signs of stress, Ackman purchased credit default swaps (CDS), which are financial instruments that pay out when a company or economy defaults on its debt. These swaps acted as a hedge against the broader market downturn. Ackman's decision to purchase credit default swaps ahead of the market crash in March 2020 proved to be one of the most successful trades of his career.

As the stock market plunged and the global economy teetered on the brink of collapse, the value of the credit default swaps skyrocketed. In just a few weeks, Pershing Square's hedge had grown to be worth more than $2.6 billion, providing a significant buffer against the losses incurred by other parts of the portfolio. Ackman's successful bet against the market in early 2020 drew widespread attention. Not only had he anticipated the severity of the pandemic's impact on the economy, but he had also acted quickly and decisively to protect his investments. This move allowed Pershing Square to not only survive the initial market crash but also capitalize on the opportunities that arose as markets began to recover.

Once the market bottomed out in late March 2020, Ackman closed his hedge and reinvested the proceeds into his core portfolio holdings, including Hilton and Chipotle, both of which rebounded strongly as the economy gradually reopened. His ability to both protect against downside risk and re-enter the market at the right time allowed Pershing Square to deliver impressive returns, even in the midst of a global crisis.

Bill Ackman's Risk Management Tactics in Volatile Times

Ackman's ability to successfully navigate financial crises is due in large part to his disciplined approach to risk management. Throughout his career, he has demonstrated an acute awareness of the risks inherent in investing and has developed strategies to mitigate those risks while maintaining the potential for outsized returns. One of Ackman's key risk management tactics is his willingness to take concentrated positions in companies he believes in while hedging those positions against broader market risks. This approach was evident in his use of credit default swaps during the COVID-19 pandemic. By purchasing these swaps, Ackman was able to protect Pershing Square's portfolio from the broader market downturn while maintaining his core investments in companies like Hilton, which he believed would ultimately recover from the crisis. Another aspect of Ackman's risk management strategy is his emphasis on thorough research and long-term thinking. Ackman is known for conducting deep, fundamental analysis on the companies he invests in, which allows him to have a high degree of conviction in his positions. This long-term perspective enables him to weather short-term volatility, as he is confident in the underlying value of his investments.

Additionally, Ackman's willingness to act quickly and decisively in times of crisis has been a hallmark of his career. Whether during the 2008 financial crisis or the COVID-19 pandemic, Ackman has shown that he is not afraid to take bold actions to protect his portfolio. His ability to recognize emerging risks early on and implement protective measures has allowed him to navigate some of the most challenging market environments. Bill Ackman's success in navigating financial crises, from the 2008 meltdown to the global pandemic in 2020, underscores his skill as a risk manager and his ability to make calculated, decisive moves in volatile times. His ability to recognize looming threats, take protective measures, and reinvest in a recovering market has enabled Pershing Square to thrive in periods of market turmoil.

Through these crises, Ackman has demonstrated that a well-constructed risk management strategy, combined with deep conviction and the willingness to act boldly, can lead to substantial success even in the most challenging market conditions.

Chapter Seven; Philosophy of Activist Investing

Bill Ackman's career is deeply intertwined with the philosophy of activist investing, a strategy that has both earned him significant returns and defined his public persona. Unlike traditional investors who may passively buy and hold stocks in the hope that a company will perform well, Ackman takes a far more involved approach. Activist investing is about taking substantial positions in companies and then pushing for changes that will unlock value.

This could include anything from replacing management to altering a company's strategic direction, or even advocating for mergers or spin-offs. For Ackman, this hands-on approach is not just a financial strategy but a way to reshape how corporations are managed and governed. Activist investing is defined by a proactive approach where an investor, usually holding a significant stake in a company, seeks to influence its decision-making processes. Unlike passive investors who rely on the board and management to steer the company, activist investors like Ackman take matters into their own hands. They often engage with the company's leadership and shareholders, advocating for operational, financial, or strategic changes. Ackman's philosophy has always been that if you see potential in a company but also identify inefficiencies or poor management, the investor should step in and propose changes that will maximize value for shareholders. Ackman chose this route because it aligns with his deeply analytical and hands-on style of investing. He recognized early in his career that many companies had hidden value that could be unlocked through strategic shifts.

Instead of waiting for management to act, Ackman believed that investors could speed up the process of value creation by directly influencing the company's decisions. His choice of activist investing also reflects his desire for control; instead of being at the mercy of market forces or waiting for corporate boards to make decisions, Ackman took on a role that allowed him to drive outcomes. This method of investing suited his personality and his belief that deep research, combined with the ability to influence outcomes, could generate superior returns.

How Ackman Reshaped Corporate Governance

One of the most significant impacts of Ackman's activist investing has been the way he has reshaped corporate governance in several companies. Corporate governance refers to the way a company is controlled and directed, including the role of shareholders, management, and the board of directors. Ackman's campaigns have often highlighted governance issues, such as the misalignment between management incentives and shareholder interests, inefficient board structures, or poor strategic decision-making.

Ackman's approach usually involves pushing for changes at the board level. In many of his campaigns, he has advocated for the replacement of board members or the addition of new directors who are more aligned with shareholder interests. His belief is that an independent, effective board can provide better oversight and hold management accountable for their decisions. This was evident in his successful campaign with Canadian Pacific Railway, where Ackman pushed for the replacement of several board members and installed new leadership that was more focused on operational efficiency. Under the new governance structure, Canadian Pacific went through a remarkable turnaround, which saw its stock price soar as operational improvements took hold. Ackman's influence on corporate governance extends beyond individual companies. His campaigns have drawn attention to broader governance issues, such as executive compensation practices and the importance of long-term thinking in corporate decision-making. His push for more shareholder-friendly governance has contributed to a shift in how boards operate, encouraging a greater focus on accountability, transparency, and alignment with investor interests.

The Power of Public Relations in Activist Campaigns

Public relations (PR) is a powerful tool in Ackman's activist campaigns. Unlike many investors who prefer to operate behind the scenes, Ackman often takes his campaigns public, using media appearances, investor presentations, and shareholder letters to make his case. He understands that by making his arguments public, he can rally other shareholders to his cause and put pressure on the company's management and board to implement the changes he is advocating. Ackman's use of PR serves multiple purposes. First, it allows him to build support for his proposals by educating other shareholders and the public about the issues he sees within a company.

For example, in his famous campaign against Herbalife, Ackman held a public presentation in which he detailed his thesis that the company was operating as a pyramid scheme. By presenting his case publicly, Ackman hoped to gain the support of regulators, other investors, and the general public in his fight against the company.

Second, PR gives Ackman leverage in negotiations with the company. By making his grievances public, he increases the pressure on management to engage with him and consider his proposals. The threat of bad publicity or shareholder revolt can often bring management to the negotiating table faster than private discussions would. However, the use of public relations can also be a double-edged sword. While it can amplify Ackman's message and help rally support, it can also backfire if the public or other shareholders disagree with his proposals. Moreover, taking a public stance can sometimes harden the company's resistance to Ackman's ideas, leading to prolonged and contentious battles, as was the case in his fight with J.C. Penney.

Key Activist Campaigns: Winners and Losers

Ackman's track record as an activist investor is marked by both notable victories and high-profile failures. His success with Canadian Pacific Railway is one of the best examples of a winning activist campaign. Ackman's push to replace the company's management and board led to a significant turnaround in its operations, making it one of the most successful railroads in North America and delivering substantial returns to Pershing Square's investors.

Another success was Ackman's campaign at Wendy's, where he pushed for the spin-off of Tim Hortons, the popular coffee chain. The spin-off unlocked significant value for Wendy's shareholders, and both companies went on to perform well independently. This campaign demonstrated Ackman's ability to identify opportunities for restructuring that could unlock hidden value within a company. On the flip side, Ackman's investment in J.C. Penney is considered one of his most high-profile failures. Despite his best efforts to transform the struggling retailer by installing a new CEO and revamping its business model, the changes alienated the company's core customers and led to disastrous financial results.

The investment ended in significant losses for Pershing Square, and Ackman eventually exited the position after failing to turn the company around. Another controversial campaign was Ackman's short position against Herbalife. Despite his public crusade against the company and efforts to prove it was a pyramid scheme, Herbalife survived regulatory scrutiny and continued to operate. Ackman's short position resulted in losses, and he eventually closed the trade after years of fighting the company.

Bill Ackman's philosophy of activist investing has reshaped how corporations operate, particularly in terms of governance and accountability. His willingness to engage in public battles and his use of PR as a strategic tool have distinguished him as a different breed of investor. While his campaigns have delivered notable victories, they have also shown the inherent risks of taking a public, confrontational approach to investing. Whether in success or failure, Ackman's campaigns have left a lasting impact on both the companies involved and the broader financial community. His approach continues to evolve, but the core philosophy of using influence to unlock value remains central to his investment strategy.

Chapter Eight; Ackman's Major Wins and Market Influence

Bill Ackman is one of the most well-known activist investors of his generation, and his influence on both individual companies and the broader financial markets is undeniable. Through Pershing Square Capital Management, Ackman has managed to deliver significant returns to his investors while simultaneously making waves in corporate governance and investment strategy.

His activist approach, which involves taking large positions in companies and pushing for changes to unlock value, has not only shaped his personal success but has also had a lasting impact on the companies he targets and the market as a whole. Pershing Square Capital Management, Ackman's hedge fund, has grown substantially since its inception in 2004. Ackman began with relatively modest capital, mostly from friends and family, but quickly built Pershing Square into one of the largest and most influential activist hedge funds in the world. A significant milestone in the fund's growth came in 2014, when Pershing Square Holdings, the publicly traded entity of the fund, was listed on the Amsterdam

Stock Exchange. This listing allowed Ackman to raise additional capital from public investors, further expanding the fund's influence. Under Ackman's leadership, Pershing Square has been known for making concentrated, high-conviction bets. While this strategy carries considerable risk, it has paid off handsomely in many cases, leading to outsized returns. Pershing Square's growth and success have also given Ackman a prominent platform from which to influence corporate strategy on a broad scale. His fund has taken major positions in companies across multiple industries, including retail, pharmaceuticals, and real estate, among others, where his input has led to significant operational and strategic changes.

Ackman's Influence on Corporate Strategy

Ackman's influence on corporate strategy has been profound. His approach typically involves taking a large stake in a company and then pushing for changes that he believes will unlock hidden value. These changes can include restructuring, operational improvements, or changes in leadership. Ackman's activism often puts him at odds with management, leading to public battles that can sometimes last for years. However, in many cases, Ackman's proposals have led to significant improvements in the companies he targets. One of the key areas where Ackman has had an impact is in reshaping corporate governance. He has frequently pushed for more shareholder-friendly practices, such as improving board independence, aligning executive compensation with shareholder interests, and increasing transparency.

Ackman's campaign with Canadian Pacific Railway is a prime example of his influence on corporate strategy. By installing new leadership and implementing operational changes, Ackman helped turn Canadian Pacific from a laggard into one of the most efficient railroads in North America, dramatically improving its financial performance and delivering substantial returns to shareholders. Ackman's influence is not limited to the companies he directly targets. His high-profile campaigns have drawn attention to the broader issue of corporate governance and the role of activist investors in driving change. Many companies have become more proactive in addressing potential shareholder concerns, knowing that they could become the next target of an activist like Ackman. This has contributed to a shift in how corporate boards operate, with an increased focus on transparency, accountability, and long-term value creation.

Notable High-Return Investments

Ackman's career is filled with notable high-return investments that have cemented his reputation as a successful activist investor. One of his most famous wins was his investment in General Growth Properties (GGP), a real estate investment trust (REIT) that owned and operated shopping malls across the United States. In 2009, as GGP faced bankruptcy during the financial crisis, Ackman took a significant position in the company, betting that it could be restructured and saved.

Through his efforts, GGP successfully emerged from bankruptcy, and Pershing Square made a profit of over $1 billion on the investment. Another high-return investment for Ackman was his involvement with Canadian Pacific Railway, where his campaign to improve operational efficiency led to a tripling of the company's stock price. This investment not only delivered substantial returns for Pershing Square's investors but also demonstrated the power of effective leadership and corporate governance in driving value. Ackman's investment in Chipotle Mexican Grill is another example of a successful campaign. In 2016, as the company struggled with food safety issues and declining sales, Ackman took a large position in the company and worked with management to improve its operations and regain customer trust.

Over time, Chipotle's stock price recovered, delivering strong returns to Ackman's fund. Ackman's investment strategy has evolved over the years, reflecting both his experiences and the changing landscape of financial markets. Early in his career, Ackman was known for making highly public, contentious activist campaigns that often involved prolonged battles with company management.

However, over time, Ackman has adopted a more collaborative approach in some cases, working behind the scenes with management teams to implement changes. This evolution reflects a recognition that not all battles need to be fought in the public eye and that constructive engagement with management can sometimes be more effective in achieving desired outcomes. One of the key aspects of Ackman's evolving strategy has been his increasing focus on risk management. While Ackman has always been willing to make bold, concentrated bets, his experiences—such as the losses incurred during his campaign with Valeant Pharmaceuticals—have taught him the importance of managing downside risk. In recent years, Ackman has implemented hedging strategies to protect his portfolio from broader market downturns, as demonstrated by his successful use of credit default swaps during the COVID-19 pandemic, which allowed him to protect Pershing Square's portfolio and generate significant returns. Another change in Ackman's approach has been his focus on long-term, sustainable investments. While his early campaigns were often aimed at driving short-term improvements in stock price, Ackman has increasingly emphasized the importance of creating long-term value for shareholders. This shift reflects a broader trend in activist investing, where the focus has moved from short-term gains to sustainable, long-term growth.

Bill Ackman's major wins, market influence, and the growth of Pershing Square Capital Management highlight his success as one of the most influential investors of his generation. His ability to influence corporate strategy, combined with his notable high-return investments, has reshaped the way companies are governed and operated. Over time, Ackman's investment strategy has evolved, reflecting his deepening understanding of risk management and the importance of long-term value creation. His impact on both individual companies and the broader market continues to be felt, solidifying his legacy as a key player in the world of activist investing.

Chapter Nine; Personal Life and Philanthropy

While Bill Ackman is widely known for his role as a hedge fund manager and activist investor, his personal life and commitment to philanthropy offer a different perspective on the man behind Pershing Square Capital Management. Ackman's life outside of finance is marked by his dedication to family, his various personal interests, and his significant philanthropic efforts.

These aspects of his life provide insight into how he balances his success in the financial world with a desire to contribute to society and make a positive impact. Bill Ackman was born into a successful business family, with his father, Lawrence Ackman, working in real estate finance. Despite his deep involvement in finance and his public persona as a high-profile investor, Ackman maintains a private and grounded personal life. Ackman has three daughters from his first marriage to landscape architect Karen Ann Herskovitz. While his marriage ended in 2017, Ackman remained close to his daughters, prioritizing family time despite his busy professional schedule. In 2019, Ackman married Neri Oxman, an architect, designer, and professor at the MIT Media Lab, who is known for her interdisciplinary work at the intersection of architecture, design, and biology.

Together, they welcomed a daughter. Ackman's family life reflects his efforts to maintain a balance between his demanding career and his personal relationships. He is a devoted father and husband, often describing his family as the anchor that keeps him grounded amid the highs and lows of the financial markets. Beyond his family life, Ackman has several personal interests and hobbies. He has a passion for architecture and design, a shared interest with his wife, Neri Oxman. Ackman has also been an avid runner, often participating in marathons, and he enjoys golf as a way to relax and unwind. His interest in sports also extends to tennis and skiing, which provide him with an outlet for both physical activity and mental relaxation. Ackman's hobbies and personal interests offer a well-rounded picture of a man who, despite his professional intensity, seeks balance and fulfillment in his personal life.

Ackman's Commitment to Charity and Philanthropy

Ackman's philanthropic efforts are a significant part of his life outside of finance. He has expressed a deep belief in the importance of using his wealth to make a meaningful difference in the world. This commitment to charity is not just a peripheral activity but an integral part of how Ackman views his responsibilities as a successful businessman.

Ackman has spoken about the impact of his upbringing on his views regarding philanthropy. His parents instilled in him a strong sense of responsibility toward helping others, which has shaped his approach to wealth and giving. For Ackman, philanthropy is not just about writing checks but about actively engaging with causes that matter to him and using his financial resources to create lasting change. One of Ackman's most significant charitable endeavors is his involvement in The Giving Pledge, an initiative founded by Warren Buffett and Bill and Melinda Gates. Through The Giving Pledge, some of the world's wealthiest individuals commit to giving away at least half of their wealth during their lifetimes or upon their deaths. Ackman's decision to join The Giving Pledge underscores his belief in the importance of wealth redistribution and his desire to use his fortune for the greater good.

The Pershing Square Foundation: Vision, Mission, and Contributions

In 2006, Bill Ackman and his then-wife Karen Ann Herskovitz established the Pershing Square Foundation, which has since become one of the primary vehicles for Ackman's philanthropic efforts. The foundation's mission is to support innovative and sustainable solutions to global challenges in areas such as education, healthcare, economic development, social justice, and the arts. The Pershing Square Foundation takes a strategic approach to philanthropy, focusing on initiatives that can create systemic change. One of the foundation's key areas of focus is education, where it has funded scholarships and educational programs aimed at providing opportunities for underserved communities. The foundation has also been a major supporter of healthcare initiatives, including funding medical research and healthcare delivery systems that can improve access to care for disadvantaged populations. In addition to education and healthcare, the Pershing Square Foundation has been active in supporting economic development programs, particularly in developing countries. The foundation believes in empowering individuals and communities through financial independence and economic opportunity, and it has funded initiatives that promote entrepreneurship, job creation, and microfinance. The foundation's commitment to social justice is also evident in its support for organizations that work to address inequality, discrimination, and human rights abuses. By funding initiatives that promote social equity, the foundation aims to create a more just and inclusive world.

Balancing Wealth with Social Responsibility

For Ackman, philanthropy is about more than just giving away money—it's about balancing the accumulation of wealth with social responsibility. He has often spoken about the moral obligation that comes with having significant financial resources, emphasizing that wealth should be used to improve the lives of others and contribute to the betterment of society. Ackman's approach to wealth and social responsibility is closely tied to his investment philosophy. Just as he takes an active role in shaping the companies he invests in, Ackman takes an active role in his philanthropic efforts, seeking out opportunities where his financial contributions can have the greatest impact. This hands-on approach to philanthropy mirrors his approach to investing, where he believes in creating value not just for himself but for a broader community.

In conclusion, Bill Ackman's personal life and philanthropic efforts reflect a man who is deeply committed to using his wealth and influence for positive change. While he is best known for his financial acumen and high-stakes investments, Ackman's dedication to family, charity, and social responsibility highlights a more personal and grounded side of his life. Through the Pershing Square Foundation and his involvement in various charitable initiatives, Ackman continues to make a meaningful impact on the world, balancing his financial success with a strong sense of social responsibility.

Chapter Ten; Criticism and Controversies

Bill Ackman's bold, high-stakes approach to investing has earned him significant financial success and a powerful presence in the business world. However, his career has not been without its share of criticism and controversies. As a high-profile activist investor, Ackman has faced accusations of market manipulation, intense media scrutiny, and public backlash from both his critics and rivals.

His public image has fluctuated dramatically over the years, with moments of both adulation and severe criticism. Throughout these ups and downs, Ackman has had to confront his mistakes and reflect on how those experiences have shaped his career. One of the most significant criticisms Ackman has faced is the accusation of market manipulation. His approach to activist investing often involves taking large positions in companies and then publicly campaigning for changes to unlock value. In some cases, Ackman has used the media and public platforms to make his case, which has led to accusations that he is trying to manipulate the market for personal gain.

A key example of these accusations came during Ackman's short-selling campaign against Herbalife in 2012. Ackman took a massive short position against the company, betting that its stock would collapse, and then publicly announced that Herbalife was a pyramid scheme. In a lengthy presentation, Ackman laid out his case, providing detailed analysis and evidence that, in his view, demonstrated that Herbalife's business model was unsustainable and illegal. Ackman predicted that the stock would go to zero as regulators shut down the company.

However, Herbalife's supporters and other market participants, including rival investor Carl Icahn, accused Ackman of trying to manipulate the stock price downward to profit from his short position. Critics argued that Ackman's public campaign was an attempt to scare investors, damage Herbalife's reputation, and benefit financially from the resulting stock decline. Herbalife itself vigorously denied Ackman's accusations, and although the company eventually settled with regulators and made changes to its business practices, it never collapsed as Ackman predicted. The public battle raised questions about the ethics of using public platforms to influence market outcomes, even if the investor believes they are acting on sound analysis.

Media Criticism and Public Backlash

Throughout his career, Ackman has faced substantial media criticism, much of which has been fueled by his willingness to take public stands on his investments. His activist campaigns are often highly visible, drawing attention not just from financial media but from mainstream outlets as well. While Ackman has garnered praise for his willingness to challenge corporate management and drive changes that create value for shareholders, he has also been criticized for the aggressive and public nature of his tactics.

One of the most notable examples of media criticism came during Ackman's battle with Carl Icahn over Herbalife. The feud between the two billionaires became a public spectacle, with both men engaging in heated exchanges on live television. Icahn accused Ackman of being a "crybaby" and a "liar," while Ackman stood by his accusations against Herbalife. The media coverage of the feud often focused more on the personal animosity between the two investors than on the merits of their respective positions, and Ackman's public image took a hit as a result. In addition to the media's focus on his battles with other investors, Ackman has also faced criticism for his investment decisions and their impact on the companies he targets. For instance, his investment in J.C. Penney, where he pushed for a radical overhaul of the company's business model, ended in disaster, with the company's sales plummeting and its stock price collapsing. The media was quick to seize on Ackman's failure, portraying him as out of touch with the realities of retail and overly confident in his ability to drive change. Ackman's high-profile losses in cases like J.C. Penney have fueled the narrative that his activism, while bold, can sometimes do more harm than good.

The Ups and Downs of Ackman's Public Image

Ackman's public image has been shaped by the high-stakes nature of his investing style. When his campaigns succeed, he is celebrated as a visionary investor who can unlock hidden value in companies and drive significant improvements in performance. However, when his campaigns fail, he is often criticized as being too aggressive, arrogant, or reckless.

For example, Ackman's successful campaign at Canadian Pacific Railway, where he pushed for a change in leadership and implemented operational improvements that led to a massive increase in shareholder value, significantly bolstered his public image. During this period, Ackman was widely praised for his foresight and his ability to turn around an underperforming company.

In contrast, his public image took a hit during the Valeant Pharmaceuticals debacle, where Ackman's investment in the company resulted in significant losses for his fund. Valeant became embroiled in scandals related to its business practices, and its stock price plummeted as regulatory scrutiny intensified. Ackman's decision to take an active role in Valeant, including joining its board of directors, tied him closely to the company's fate.

When Valeant failed to recover, Ackman's public image suffered, with many questioning his judgment and his ability to properly assess risk. These ups and downs have made Ackman a polarizing figure in the financial world. To his supporters, he is a brilliant investor who has the courage to take on tough battles and challenge the status quo. To his critics, he is an opportunist who uses his influence to manipulate markets and take unnecessary risks.

Reflecting on Mistakes and Learning from Failures

Throughout his career, Ackman has had to confront the fact that not all of his investments will succeed. His high-profile failures, such as J.C. Penney and Valeant, have provided valuable lessons that have shaped his approach to investing over time. One of the key lessons Ackman has learned is the importance of risk management.

The substantial losses he incurred in Valeant, in particular, underscored the need for a more disciplined approach to managing concentrated positions and ensuring that thorough due diligence is conducted before making large investments. Ackman has also acknowledged that some of his past campaigns may have been too aggressive or ambitious. For example, in reflecting on his campaign at JCPenney, Ackman has admitted that the changes he pushed for may have been too radical and that he underestimated the challenges of turning around a struggling retailer. This experience has influenced his approach to future campaigns, making him more cautious about pushing for sweeping changes without fully understanding the potential consequences.

Despite these setbacks, Ackman has remained committed to his philosophy of activist investing. He views his failures as opportunities to learn and refine his strategies, and his willingness to reflect on his mistakes has helped him recover from difficult periods and continue to thrive in the world of finance.

Bill Ackman's career has been marked by both triumphs and controversies, with accusations of market manipulation and intense media scrutiny shaping his public image. While he has faced criticism for his aggressive activist campaigns and high-profile failures, Ackman's ability to reflect on his mistakes and learn from them has allowed him to remain a significant force in the financial world. His career serves as a reminder that even the most successful investors will encounter setbacks, but those who can adapt and grow from their experiences are the ones who will continue to succeed in the long run.

Chapter Eleven; Bill Ackman's Legacy and Future

Bill Ackman has cemented his place as one of the most influential and audacious figures in modern finance. His unique blend of bold activism, high-stakes investment strategies, and willingness to challenge conventional corporate governance has left an indelible mark on the financial world. As his career continues to evolve, the long-term impact of his contributions is becoming clearer.

His influence is not only seen in the companies he has targeted but also in the broader financial strategies that other investors have adopted in response to his groundbreaking tactics. Ackman's legacy is already shaping the future of finance, as well as the next generation of activist investors, and his future with Pershing Square remains highly anticipated by many. Bill Ackman's impact on the financial world extends beyond the significant returns his hedge fund has generated or the companies he has engaged with through activist investing. One of his most lasting contributions has been his role in popularizing and redefining activist investing. Ackman demonstrated that investors could not only identify undervalued companies but also actively engage in improving their operations, reshaping their governance, and driving long-term value for shareholders. This shift encouraged other hedge funds and institutional investors to take a more hands-on approach to managing their investments.

Ackman's campaigns have also had a transformative effect on corporate governance. He has frequently pushed for increased accountability, transparency, and alignment between management incentives and shareholder value. Companies that have been subject to Ackman's activism, such as Canadian Pacific Railway and Chipotle, have undergone significant operational improvements under his guidance. This has encouraged corporate boards and executives across industries to be more proactive in addressing governance issues, fearing that failure to do so could make them targets of activist investors like Ackman. Furthermore, Ackman's ability to blend financial analysis with public relations has shifted how activist investors communicate their intentions. His use of detailed presentations, media appearances, and public advocacy has become a template for other activist investors who want to rally shareholder support and push for corporate change. In this way, Ackman has not only changed how companies operate but also how the financial world interacts with and influences corporate decision-making.

What's Next for Pershing Square and Bill Ackman

Looking ahead, Pershing Square and Bill Ackman continue to be key players in the hedge fund world. Ackman's firm remains one of the largest and most influential activist investment vehicles globally, and it is expected that the fund will continue to identify opportunities for corporate intervention and long-term value creation. As Pershing Square has evolved, so too has Ackman's strategy, becoming more balanced between high-conviction bets and risk management.

His successful hedge against the COVID-19 pandemic in 2020 demonstrated a more cautious and adaptive approach, signaling that Ackman is focused on navigating future market volatility with greater precision. In terms of where Ackman might direct Pershing Square's attention in the future, it is likely that he will continue to target underperforming or undervalued companies where there is potential for operational improvements. Ackman has increasingly shown interest in companies that are not just profitable but also have the potential to contribute positively to society—aligning his activism with broader societal goals. This could mean more investments in areas like green technology, healthcare, and companies that are aligned with environmental, social, and governance (ESG) principles. In addition to his continued role at Pershing Square, Ackman is likely to expand his influence through his philanthropic endeavors. The Pershing Square Foundation, which he co-founded, has already committed substantial resources to various social causes. As Ackman's wealth grows, his role as a philanthropist will likely take on an even greater dimension, allowing him to influence areas outside of finance, from education to healthcare, in meaningful ways.

Reflections on a Career Full of High Stakes

Ackman's career has been defined by high-stakes decisions and moments of intense public scrutiny. From his highly publicized short position on Herbalife to his battles with J.C. Penney and his successes with Canadian Pacific Railway, Ackman has never shied away from risk. His willingness to stake his reputation and vast sums of money on his investment convictions has drawn both admiration and criticism. Reflecting on his career, Ackman's biggest successes have come when he has stayed true to his rigorous analysis and long-term vision. His campaign with Canadian Pacific, for example, exemplified how deep research and a strategic vision for operational improvement could turn around an underperforming company. Similarly, his investment in General Growth Properties during the financial crisis showcased his ability to identify hidden value in distressed companies.

On the flip side, Ackman has learned hard lessons from his failures, particularly from his ill-fated investment in Valeant Pharmaceuticals. The Valeant experience, in which Ackman's bet on the company turned disastrous due to scandals and accounting issues, was a humbling moment that reminded Ackman of the importance of thorough due diligence and managing the risks associated with concentrated positions. Ultimately, Ackman's career has been defined not just by his wins and losses but by his resilience and willingness to learn from his mistakes. His ability to reflect on these experiences has enabled him to adapt his strategy over time, becoming a more balanced and thoughtful investor in the process.

The Legacy of Ackman's Investment Strategies for Future Generations

Bill Ackman's legacy will be felt by future generations of investors who see activism not as a short-term play but as a long-term strategy for value creation. Ackman has proven that activist investing can be a powerful force for good when used to improve companies and align management with shareholder interests. His campaigns have shown that thoughtful, research-driven activism can generate both financial returns and positive operational changes for companies.

For future investors, Ackman's career serves as a blueprint for how to manage risk while still pursuing bold, high-conviction investments. His use of hedging strategies, particularly during times of crisis like the 2020 pandemic, provides valuable lessons in risk management. Future generations of investors will likely draw from Ackman's example, understanding that the best returns often come when investors are both bold and prudent, combining conviction with calculated risk mitigation. Moreover, Ackman's legacy will be remembered for his willingness to challenge entrenched corporate practices and push for better governance. He has been a force for change in the financial world, showing that investors have the power to hold companies accountable and drive them to perform at their best. For the next wave of investors, Ackman's career will serve as a guide for how to balance profitability with ethical considerations, demonstrating that financial success and social responsibility can go hand in hand.

Bill Ackman's legacy in the financial world is far-reaching, encompassing his role as a pioneer in activist investing, his significant influence on corporate governance, and his ability to navigate high-stakes financial markets with both success and failure. His continued leadership at Pershing Square and his growing philanthropic commitments signal that his influence will persist for years to come. Future generations of investors will undoubtedly look to Ackman's career for guidance, drawing lessons from his investment strategies, his resilience, and his commitment to making a lasting impact both in finance and beyond.

Conclusion

Bill Ackman's influence on the hedge fund world is undeniable. As one of the most prominent activist investors of his generation, Ackman has not only generated significant returns but also fundamentally reshaped the relationship between investors and the companies they hold stakes in. His unique approach, which involves deep research, public advocacy, and strategic activism, has set a new standard for how investors can engage with underperforming companies and unlock hidden value.

Ackman's impact extends far beyond the financial returns he has achieved, influencing corporate governance and the broader landscape of hedge fund investing. Ackman's financial journey has been marked by both triumphs and failures, each of which has offered valuable lessons. One of the key takeaways from Ackman's career is the importance of conviction. Whether he was betting against MBIA during the 2008 financial crisis or campaigning for changes at Canadian Pacific Railway, Ackman's success has often come from his unwavering belief in his research and strategy. However, Ackman's journey has also shown the importance of adaptability. His willingness to learn from mistakes, such as his high-profile failures with J.C. Penney and Valeant Pharmaceuticals, has allowed him to refine his approach over time and emerge stronger from setbacks. Bill Ackman's legacy in the world of activist investing is profound. He has demonstrated that activism, when done thoughtfully, can create long-term value for both shareholders and the companies themselves.

Ackman changed the game by showing that activist investors could be more than just corporate raiders—he introduced a model where activism was paired with deep analysis, strategic planning, and a public campaign to win support from other investors. Ackman also helped popularize the idea that investors should not simply hold management accountable but work with them to improve operations and governance. In conclusion, Bill Ackman's financial journey has redefined what it means to be an activist investor. His strategies, successes, and even failures have left an indelible mark on the hedge fund industry, showing that bold, activist investing can lead to significant positive change, both financially and operationally, for companies and shareholders alike.

www.ingramcontent.com/pod-product-compliance
Ingram Content Group UK Ltd.
Pitfield, Milton Keynes, MK11 3LW, UK
UKHW041641190726
13854UKWH00006B/2637

9 798330 397587